IMAGES OF SHEFFIELD

GEOFFREY HOWSE

SUTTON PUBLISHING

Sutton Publishing Limited
Phoenix Mill · Thrupp · Stroud
Gloucestershire · GL5 2BU

First published 2005

Copyright © Geoffrey Howse, 2005

Title page photograph: Coat of arms of the
City of Sheffield. *(Author's Collection)*

British Library Cataloguing in Publication Data
A catalogue record for this book is available from the
British Library.

ISBN 0-7509-3502-2

Typeset in 10.5/13.5pt Photina.
Typesetting and origination by
Sutton Publishing Limited.
Printed and bound in England by
J.H. Haynes & Co. Ltd, Sparkford.

This Edwardian postcard was published by M. Smith General Stores, Ecclesfield. It is captioned 'Council Hall, Ecclesfield'. The historic village of Ecclesfield, with its magnificent St Mary's Church (known as 'the Minster of the Moors', seen in the background), whose parish once covered 78 square miles, lies about 5 miles north-east of Sheffield. The building seen here, with its gables and mullioned windows, was better known as the Feoffees Hall. A feoffee was a member of a board of trustees who administered land for charitable public purposes. The history of the feoffees in Ecclesfield, of which there were originally fourteen, dates back to 1549. The Feoffees Hall was built in the 1730s as a workhouse. It ceased to be used as such after the Wortley Union Workhouse opened at Grenoside in 1852. The building was used as a school until 1894, and from 1895 to 1930 for Parish Council meetings. It was demolished in 1968. *(Author's Collection)*

CONTENTS

Yorkshireman's Coat of Arms.

Here's tiv us. all on us,
May we niver want nowt, noan on us,
Nor me nawther.

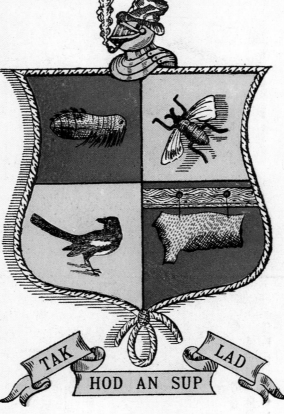

QUI
CAPIT
IL
HABET

COP
T'LOT
AN
STICK

TAK   LAD

HOD AN SUP

A flea, a fly, a magpie, an' t' bacon flitch
'as allus been t Yorkshireman's crest
An' t' reason o' this is plain to be seen
for, like him, they're all o' the best.
A flea will bite whoivver it can –
an' soa, by gow, will a Yorkshireman!
A fly will sup with Teddy or Dan –
an' soa an' all will a Yorkshireman!
A magpie can chelp for a terrible span—
an' soa, my lads, can a Yorkshireman!
A flitch whol it s hung 's noa gooid y ell agree—
no more is a Yorkshireman doant yer see.

This amusing Edwardian postcard depicts a Yorkshireman's imaginary coat of arms, accompanied by a suitably tongue-in-cheek doggerel verse. (*Author's Collection*)

INTRODUCTION

Sheffield, with a population exceeding half a million, is England's fourth largest city and was built on seven hills and five river valleys. Its rivers played an important part in the development of the industries for which Sheffield has become world renowned. The rivers are the Don, the Sheaf, the Rivelin, the Loxley and the Porter. A wealth of parks in the city and throughout its catchment area, combined with considerable tracts of ancient woodland, open fields and the fact that a third of its boundaries lie within the Peak District National Park, makes Sheffield the greenest city in the country. First-time visitors to Sheffield with the preconceived notion that they will be surrounded by dust and grime are often shocked, and pleasantly surprised when they realise it is one of the cleanest industrial cities in the whole of Europe.

A settlement existed in what became known as Sheffield long before the Romans came to Britain. They built a road into Derbyshire and a fort at Wincobank. In 829 the Anglian kings of Northumberland and Mercia met at Dore to settle their differences. The area within the ancient manor of Hallam, and the region known as Hallamshire which includes Sheffield and district is a historic one, and much has been written about the development of various communities here. The Normans built a castle on the site now occupied by Castle Market. This was replaced by another. Early lords in the late Middle Ages in Hallamshire were the Furnivals. A reminder of that family is the area known as Furnival Gate in the city centre (see p. 50). The male line of the Furnival family came to an end towards the close of the fourteenth century. Early in the fifteenth century the Talbots became established in Sheffield, after John Talbot, the owner of considerable lands in Shropshire, had married Maud Nevill, daughter and heiress of Sir Thomas Nevill and Joan de Furnival. The Talbot family dominated the area for over 200 years from their castle in Sheffield and their Manor Lodge. Only fragments of Sheffield Castle remain beneath today's Castle Market, but there are more substantial remains of Manor Lodge. This was originally a hunting lodge in the old deer park, and had been in use since at least the beginning of the last quarter of the fifteenth century. The first of the Talbots, John, served in Ireland as Lord Lieutenant from 1414 to 1419 and took charge of the English army in France in 1428. His military achievements earned him high honours: first he was created Knight of the Garter, and in 1442 he was raised to the peerage as the Earl of Shrewsbury.

The 1st Earl of Shrewsbury died in battle in France in 1453. His son, the 2nd Earl, died in the Battle of Northampton in 1460. The first three earls of Shrewsbury did not spend much time on what they regarded as one of their lesser estates. It was

George Talbot, the 4th Earl (1468–1538), who decided to make his principal home in Sheffield. He did not consider Sheffield Castle fashionable enough and set about improving his hunting lodge, upgrading it to a substantial country house. In 1530 Cardinal Wolsey spent eighteen days there. He died four days after his visit, at Leicester. On the 4th Earl's death his body was buried in Sheffield parish church, in the chapel he had built (still known as the Shrewsbury Chapel) in today's cathedral church of St Peter and St Paul. Francis, the 5th Earl, was born at Sheffield Castle in 1500. He occupied various important positions including President of the Council of the North, and was a member of the Privy Council at the court of Elizabeth I. He continued to build at Sheffield Lodge and exerted a great deal of influence locally. George Talbot, the 6th Earl (*c.* 1528–90), became even more powerful than his predecessors: he was a member of the Privy Council, Lieutenant-General of Yorkshire, Nottinghamshire and Derbyshire, and, following the execution of the Duke of Norfolk in 1572, Earl Marshal of England. He married twice, his second wife being that celebrated Elizabethan Bess of Hardwick (1527–1608). On his marriage to Bess in 1567, becoming her fourth husband, he acquired a life interest in Chatsworth House but despite having large estates in eleven counties and London, which included three castles, Sheffield Manor Lodge remained his favourite seat, and he and his wife spent a great deal of money enlarging it and improving the gardens.

An early twentieth-century view of the sixteenth-century Turret House, Manor Castle, the only part of the once extensive Manor Lodge, one time seat of the earls of Shrewsbury and place of incarceration of Mary Queen of Scots, to survive intact. The Turret House dates from 1574. (*Author's Collection*)

An early postcard showing Bishop's House, situated in Meersbrook Park, Norton Lees Lane, about 2 miles south of Sheffield city centre. This fine example of a properous yeoman's residence dates from the late fifteenth century and has sixteenth- and seventeenth-century additions. It is the earliest timber-framed house still standing in Sheffield. After extensive renovation the house was opened as a museum in 1976. (*Author's Collection*)

After the arrest of Mary Queen of Scots in 1569, Elizabeth I appointed her loyal subject George, 6th Earl of Shrewsbury, as her custodian. The Queen of Scots was brought to Sheffield and remained in his charge from 1570 to 1584. She was mainly imprisoned at Sheffield Castle and Sheffield Manor Lodge but from time to time was moved to Buxton or Chatsworth and once to Worksop. During this long period of incarceration the marriage of the Earl and Bess broke down and they lived apart until the Earl's death in 1590, when Bess once again gained full control of her estates. She outlived her husband by seventeen years. George's son Gilbert (1553 –1616) succeeded him as the 7th Earl. He became a prominent figure at court.

After Gilbert died, having had no sons, and his only brother dying soon afterwards, the title passed to a distant relative. Gilbert's estates were shared between his three daughters. The youngest inherited the Yorkshire and Derbyshire properties. She married Thomas Howard, Earl of Arundel and Surrey. Her grandson was created the 5th Duke of Norfolk (the Howards having forfeited that title in 1572), and subsequent dukes of Norfolk have had close links with Sheffield to this day. Shortly after the Howards inherited their estates in Yorkshire Sheffield Castle was completely destroyed on the instructions of Parliament in 1649–50, when all castles that had been defended by Royalists during the Civil War had to be demolished. The Manor

St Mary's Church, Handsworth, *c.* 1905. The chancel, north chapel and the lower part of the tower date from the thirteenth century but most of the rest dates from the nineteenth. The octagonal tower top and the spire were added in 1825, the north aisle in 1833 and the south aisle in 1904. *(Chris Sharp of Old Barnsley)*

Lodge fell into disrepair. Most of what remained of this once spectacular mansion was dismantled in the early eighteenth century.

The close proximity of plentiful supplies of water and rich beds of iron ore were responsible for the growth of cutlery manufacture and the iron and steel industry in Sheffield. Early industry was quick to make use of the rivers as a source of power. Scores of dams were built in the river valleys, which held water to turn hundreds of water wheels. Timber was readily available and this was turned into charcoal for the smelting and forging industries. Coal provided energy during the Industrial Revolution but it was water power which made Sheffield famous for cutlery production. By the fourteenth century it seems Sheffield was already well known for cutlery production, when Geoffrey Chaucer (c. 1340–1400) in his *Canterbury Tales* mentions 'A Sheffield thwitel [whittler] baar he in his hose'.

From the earliest times the majority of metalworking was done by farmers from the nearby villages, who worked part-time, usually from home, and would rent time on one of the water-powered wheels or hammers. The hills in and around Sheffield made transportation of goods difficult, so specialised industries sprang up in areas where goods could be carried by horse or on foot. The villages to the south of Sheffield, around Abbeydale and Norton, made scythes and sickles, whereas to the north, in Ecclesfield and Grenoside, nail and file making were the main industries. The cutlers worked principally in the town, along the banks of the River Don. The Cutlers' Company was set up in 1624 as a guild of craftsmen.

By 1700 crude steel was being made in Sheffield, and in 1724 Benjamin Huntsman invented a way of melting blister steel in clay pots to make crucible steel, a high-quality steel which remained the best available for over a hundred years. Production of such excellent steel in large quantities was made possible when in 1858 Henry Bessemer brought his 'converter' to Sheffield. Expansion of the steel and cutlery industries was rapid during the Industrial Revolution; in the closing years of the eighteenth century the first factories were built, using steam engines to drive the machinery.

The opening of Sheffield Canal in 1819 and the coming of the railway in 1837 meant that raw materials could be more easily brought into Sheffield and manufactured goods exported. The development of the railways and the need for enormous quantities of high-quality steel saw further expansion in Sheffield. By the 1880s the town was producing 'special steels' and development continued.

Sheffield was granted a City Charter in 1893. In 1905 Sheffield University was opened by King Edward VII and Queen Alexandra. The old parish church was raised to cathedral status in 1914, with Leonard Hedley Burrows as the first bishop. The previous year, Harry Brearley of Sheffield discovered that by mixing chromium with steel the metal would not corrode. He had invented stainless steel. Today, modern production methods mean that comparatively few local people work in the cutlery or steel industries, but Sheffield is still famous for those industries the world over.

One major advantage in having such diversity of heavy industry within one area has been the growth of unrivalled medical facilities. Research into various industrial and other illnesses at Sheffield's numerous medical institutions has resulted in the city being blessed with some of the finest teaching hospitals in the United Kingdom.

Sheffield is a city of sport. It already had an enviable sporting record in staging events before the Sports Council named it Britain's first National City of Sport in 1995. Soccer was born in Sheffield. Sheffield FC, founded on 24 October 1857, is the world's oldest football club. Matches were first played between teams made up of club members. Sheffield produced the first soccer rule book when the area had fifteen teams. In 1877 an agreement was made between the London Association and the Sheffield Association to use the same rules, which formed the basis of the rules still in use today.

In this, my sixth book about Sheffield and the area surrounding this great city, I have attempted to include a wide range of images which both capture the spirit and show the diversity of this truly remarkable area. I have collected postcard views, which account for approximately 70 per cent of the images used, some of which are of unusual subjects, many of them published during the heyday of the picture postcard. The world's first official postcard was issued by Austria on 1 October 1869. A year later the Post Office introduced the first official postcards in Britain. No pictures were allowed on these early postcards. but restrictions were lifted when the rule imposed by the Post Office that a postcard had to carry a printed prepaid stamp was changed. From 1 September 1894, privately printed postcards were allowed to be sent through the post with an adhesive halfpenny stamp. One of the earliest known picture postcards to be sent in Britain was of Scarborough and franked 15 September 1894. It was published by E.T.W. Dennis of Scarborough. Picture postcards soon became a very popular form of communication and many of the images of Sheffield and district included here show how even the most ordinary streetscape or pastoral scene could become a picture postcard. Often the message on the postcard or the postal marks are more interesting than the view. A considerable number of the postcards dating from 1895 until at least the beginning of the First World War appear to have been sent by, or to, young women in service; either to show family members the area in which they were working, or as a memento of life back home. In some instances there is more than one view of the same subject, which illustrates just how popular postcards were. As well as views of the city centre, Sheffield's industries and the towns and villages scattered throughout the area, I have also included many images of Sheffield's parks and beauty spots, popular subjects for the picture postcard publisher. I hope readers will find my selection an interesting one.

Geoffrey Howse, June 2005

1

The Cathedral & Environs

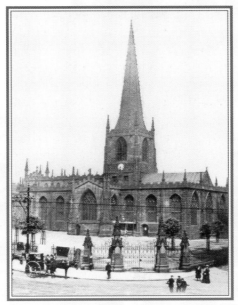

A late Victorian postcard showing Sheffield parish church, touchingly inscribed 'from Mother to her boy'. *(Author's Collection)*

An early view of St Peter's, Sheffield's parish church. Most of the old cruciform church dates from the first half of the fifteenth century. It was restored in the late eighteenth century and again in 1880. *(Author's Collection)*

This postcard view of Sheffield parish church was posted in Eckington and franked 8pm, 17 September 1909. Sent in the days when local post offices had a greater knowledge of their residents, it is addressed simply to Mrs Mathers, Willoughton, Nr Lincoln. *(Author's Collection)*

One of the Valentine series of postcards produced shortly after Sheffield's ancient parish church was raised to cathedral status in 1914. *(Author's Collection)*

The Shrewsbury Chapel, Cathedral Church of St Peter and St Paul, *c.* 1920. *(Sheffield Central Library)*

Church Street, 1903. The carriages and cabs on the left are parked outside St Peter's Church. On the right is the Cutlers' Hall, the home of the Cutlers' Company. It is the third building to be constructed for the Cutlers' Company on the same site. It was erected in 1832 to the designs of Samuel Worth and B.B. Taylor, and extended in 1881. The Cutlers' Company was incorporated by Act of Parliament in 1624 to regulate the cutlery industry. The Cutlers' Hall is the setting for the annual celebration of Sheffield's manufacturing industry, the Cutlers' Feast. Cole Brothers' Fargate store can be seen to the left of the Cutlers' Hall with High Street beyond. *(David J. Richardson Collection)*

A view from the same spot as the picture above, July 2000. A supertram can be seen on the left. *(Paul T. Langley Welch)*

This view of Cole's Corner was sent to Nottingham on 1 March 1907 and taken from the junction of Fargate with High Street and Church Street. This popular department store was founded by three brothers in 1847. The building seen here was constructed in the 1860s and Cole's Corner became a popular meeting place. In September 1963 Cole Brothers moved to new premises in Barker's Pool, after which their old store was demolished. Church Street can be seen to the right. *(Author's Collection)*

Another Edwardian view of Cole's Corner and Fargate. This postcard was sent to Hull on 21 September 1907. *(Author's Collection)*

Cole's Corner and Fargate before the First World War. *(Author's Collection)*

Cole's Corner in 1963. *(David J. Richardson Collection)*

The site of Cole Brothers' department store, July 2000. Cole's Corner is now occupied by the HSBC Bank.
(Paul T. Langley Welch)

This Edwardian postcard shows Cole Brothers' department store and the shops on the north side of Fargate. *(Author's Collection)*

This pre-1900 postcard showing Fargate was taken from Pinfold Street. The Albany Hotel can be seen on the right. Produced by Valentine's, the card is franked 14 February 1905. *(Author's Collection)*

Fargate and Leopold Street, from the junction of Pinstone Street and Barker's Pool, 1900. *(David J. Richardson Collection)*

An Edwardian postcard view of Fargate, franked 14 September 1907. When one compares the three images seen on this page, it is interesting to note the changes that have taken place over a relatively short time span. *(Author's Collection)*

A view of Fargate and Leopold Street, July 2000. Compare this with the three images on the opposite page. *(Paul T. Langley Welch)*

A pre-First World War postcard view of Fargate. *(Author's Collection)*

A view from Town Hall Square, Fargate, *c.* 1960. *(Author's Collection)*

Fargate, photographed by J.F. Lawrence in the early 1950s. *(Author's Collection)*

Fargate, seen from the same spot as the picture above, July 2000. *(Paul T. Langley Welch)*

The south side of Fargate, 1920. Hanbidge's shop is at the junction of Norfolk Row. *(David J. Richardson Collection)*

The south side of Fargate, July 2000. Next now occupies the site where Hanbidge's once stood. *(Paul T. Langley Welch)*

A magnificent view of Fargate from a high vantage point in Town Hall Square, during the 1930s. The impressive Sheffield Telegraph building, built in 1913, can be seen in the centre, at the end of Fargate in High Street. (*Author's Collection*)

A 1970s postcard view of Barker's Pool. The corner of Cole Brothers' department store, which moved from Fargate to these new premises in 1963, can be seen on the right. Sheffield City Hall is seen in the left foreground. It opened on 22 September 1932. Barker's Pool dates back as far as 1435, when a Mr Barker built a reservoir, which existed until 1793. The City War Memorial was designed by Charles Carus Wilson, architect, and sculpted by George Alexander. The memorial's bronze base is 17ft 6in high and 6ft 6in in diameter. Four slightly smaller than lifesize figures of servicemen from the navy, merchant navy, army and air force stand above panels displaying the arms of the City of Sheffield and the emblems of local regiments. A white flagpole made of mild steel rises above the sculpted portion of the war memorial. The memorial was unveiled by Lt-Gen Sir Charles H. Harington GBE, KCB, DSO, on 28 October 1925. (*Author's Collection*)

A late 1960s postcard showing Goodwin Fountain and behind it Wilson Peck, the music store, situated at the corner of Leopold Street and Barker's Pool. *(Author's Collection)*

2

High Street

High Street seen from Sheffield parish church in 1863.
(David J. Richardson Collection)

High Street, from the corner of Fargate, 1892. One of Sheffield's oldest streets, High Street was originally a link between the medieval castle and the parish church. Parts of the old High Street were only 20ft wide. In the closing years of the nineteenth century street widening began and many buildings were demolished. *(David J. Richardson Collection)*

A slightly later nineteenth-century image, from a similar viewpoint. W. Foster & Son, whose advertising sign boasts that they are the 'Oldest Clothiers in the City' is at 8 High Street and W. Lewis's tobacconists is at no. 6. Some time after 1892 the two upper storeys of the part of Foster's shop that lies to the right of the main building were demolished. Shortly after this photograph was taken many of the buildings seen here were taken down to facilitate the widening of High Street. *(David J. Richardson Collection)*

An early Edwardian postcard featuring the High Street, again from a similar viewpoint to the previous two images. Some buildings have been set back in the extensive rebuilding programme that had recently been undertaken. *(Author's Collection)*

High Street. This postcard is franked 10 November 1910. The building that juts out slightly in the left background is Fitzalan Market, situated at the top of Angel Street at its junction with High Street. *(Author's Collection)*

High Street from Cole's Corner at the bottom of Fargate, 1936. More demolition and rebuilding has taken place, the Sheffield Telegraph building, constructed in 1913, being the most notable example of a major change to the streetscape. *(Author's Collection)*

A 1940s postcard of High Street, franked 27 October 1949. *(Author's Collection)*

High Street, July 2000. Above the main entrance of what was once the Sheffield Telegraph building is emblazoned Bradford & Bingley. This eye-catching High Street landmark now houses a building society. *(Paul T. Langley Welch)*

High Street in 1905, looking towards Cole's Corner. Cole Brothers' department store can be seen centre left and beyond it the Cutlers' Hall. In the left foreground is the department store established by John Walsh in 1896. The latter was destroyed during the Sheffield Blitz in December 1940. Walsh's new store opened in 1953 on the site of their old building; in the 1970s it became Rackhams, and in the 1980s, House of Fraser. After its closure in 1998 the premises were taken over by T.J. Hughes. *(David J. Richardson Collection)*

High Street, 12 July 1905. Walsh's store is decorated for the visit of King Edward VII and Queen Alexandra for the opening of Sheffield University. *(David J. Richardson Collection)*

High Street, looking from the top of Angel Street towards Cole's Corner, *c.* 1912. *(Author's Collection)*

From 1967 until 1994 Sheffield boasted the most extensive network of subterranean tunnels or subways in any English city. Castle Square, more popularly known as the 'hole in the road', was an especially fine example of modernist city architecture. From a purely practical point of view the subways enabled shoppers to gain access at basement level to several department stores and shops, and Castle Square in particular provided a meeting point and a pleasantly appointed place to relax for a few minutes while shopping; and to enjoy watching the fish displayed in a large tank. Although Castle Square was a short-lived feature, it is still fondly remembered. In May 1994 the 'hole in the road' was filled in, in preparation for the laying of the tram lines for the supertram. The city centre streetscape has sacrificed one of its most innovative features and Sheffield is the poorer for it. *(Sheffield Central Library)*

High Street and Castle Square from the opposite side, July 2000. Walsh's old department store is now occupied by T.J. Hughes. *(Author's Collection)*

High Street from the junction of Commercial Street with Fitzalan Square, 1930s. The spire of the cathedral can be seen in the centre background. *(Author's Collection)*

An early 1960s postcard view taken from a slightly higher vantage point than the image above and showing Walsh's department store centre left. *(Author's Collection)*

This early 1960s postcard, franked 20 July 1965, shows the bottom of High Street and Commercial Street. It was taken from a high vantage point at the corner of Angel Street. *(Author's Collection)*

3

Fitzalan Square, Angel Street & Haymarket

The General Post Office, Fitzalan Square, at its junction with Pond Street, *c.* 1915.
(Author's Collection)

Fitzalan Square, 1902. This square is situated at the bottom of High Street at its junction with Commercial Street and Haymarket. The name is derived from a branch of the Howard family, Howard being the family name of the dukes of Norfolk. This open space was created in 1881 on the site of buildings that had been demolished in Market Street. The Fitzalan Market Hall can be seen across the square with Haymarket to its right. *(David J. Richardson Collection)*

An 1890s postcard featuring Fitzalan Square. *(Author's Collection)*

Fitzalan Square twenty years later. *(Author's Collection)*

The opposite side of Fitzalan Square. The General Post Office can be seen centre back. This postcard is franked 28 September 1918. (*Author's Collection*)

This Fitzalan Square postcard is franked 21 September 1948. (*Author's Collection*)

This postcard image of Fitzalan Square was sent to his parents by Peter Wake in 1948. *(Author's Collection)*

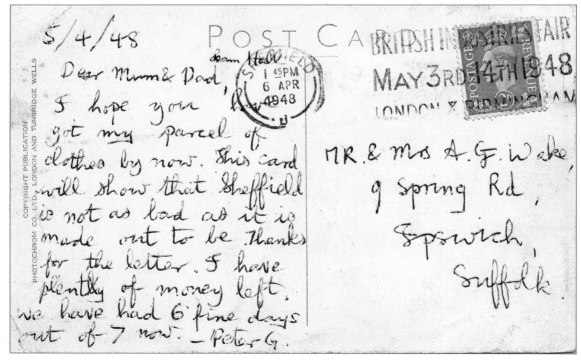

The reverse of the postcard above. Judging by Peter Wake's comments, Sheffield held some appeal for him. *(Author's Collection)*

Fitzalan Square in the 1970s. *(Author's Collection)*

Fitzalan Square, seen here from a similar spot. Mature trees now mask much of the view across the square from all directions. *(Paul T. Langley Welch)*

Market Place and Angel Street, 1895. In the right foreground at the junction of High Street is Fitzalan Market. Fitzalan Market opened in 1786, the original building being replaced in 1864 by the one seen here. This market specialised in meat and fish. The corn market was held each Tuesday on the High Street side. The building closed on 24 April 1930 and was demolished in 1931. *(David J. Richardson Collection)*

Left: Cockaynes store at 1 Angel Street, 1900. The store was founded by two brothers, Thomas B. and William Cockayne as a general drapers. The firm expanded and during the twentieth century the five-storey shop seen here was selling a wide range of goods. Cockaynes was destroyed in December 1940 during the Sheffield Blitz. *(David J. Richardson Collection)*
Right: The site of Cockaynes store, seen here in July 2000. Cockaynes traded here after the Second World War, until the shop was taken over by Schofields. The entire premises are now occupied by the Argos superstore. *(Paul T. Langley Welch)*

An Edwardian postcard
showing Angel Street.
(*Author's Collection*)

Above: This Edwardian
image of Angel Street
remained in circulation for
several decades. This
particular card was
published by John Walsh
Ltd, and was posted to Rye
in Sussex on 25 February
1958. (*Author's Collection*)

Right: Market Place and
Angel Street, illustrated on a
postcard of *c*. 1912.
(*Author's Collection*)

A bootblack plies his trade in Commercial Street, *c.* 1900. *(David J. Richardson Collection)*

4

Around the Town Hall & the Moor

A 1905 postcard featuring Sheffield town hall.
(Author's Collection)

The old town hall in Waingate had served Sheffield since 1808. With an ever-increasing population it was decided that Sheffield required a more opulent building. The new town hall was designed by E.W. Mountford and built at a cost of £80,000. Construction began in 1891 and continued until 1896. The new town hall was officially opened by Her Majesty Queen Victoria on 21 May 1897. This late Victorian card shows it shortly after its official opening. The obelisk seen in the foreground, sited at the junction of Fargate and Leopold Street, is the Jubilee Memorial of 1887, designed by Flockton & Gibbs. The monument stood approximately 33ft high, and consisted of a block of grey polished granite surmounted by a carved stone capital, topped with an obelisk of red polished granite. It was surrounded by four cast-iron gas lamps. The granite base bore the inscription, 'Erected to commemorate the jubilee of Queen Victoria 1887'. The Jubilee Memorial was moved to Endcliffe Park in 1905. It was replaced by a statue of Queen Victoria in the same year. (*Author's Collection*)

Sheffield town hall, 1907. The statue of Queen Victoria replaced the Jubilee Memorial. The approximately 10ft high statue, by Alfred Turner, is of bronze and stands on top of a plinth of limestone blocks. It bears the date 1904, although it was not put in place until the following year. The statue was unveiled by Princess Beatrice of Battenburg on 11 May 1905. Like its predecessor the Jubilee Memorial, this statue was also moved to Endcliffe Park in 1930. (*David J. Richardson Collection*)

This postcard of Sheffield town hall was sent to Margate on 29 July 1913. *(Author's Collection)*

A pre-1930 postcard showing a busy Town Hall Square, taken on St George's Day. *(Author's Collection)*

This late nineteenth-century postcard shows St Paul's Church in all its magnificence, and beyond it Sheffield's newly built town hall. The Jubilee Memorial can just be glimpsed in the bottom left-hand corner. The spire of the Catholic St Marie's Church in Norfolk Row can be seen above the roof of St Paul's. The first stone of the baroque St Paul's Church, arguably the City of Sheffield's finest Georgian building, was laid on 28 May 1720 and was built as a chapel-of-ease to the nearby medieval parish church of St Peter. St Paul's, Pinstone Street, was built to the designs of Ralph Tunnicliffe of Dalton, assisted by John Platt the elder. The dome on top of the tower was added in 1769. Sheffield was an archdeaconry within the diocese of York from 1884. After the raising of the parish church to cathedral status in 1914, and owing to a shift of population from the city centre to the suburbs, many city churches became redundant. In 1936 it was decided that some had to be demolished, and St Paul's was one of them. The Peace Gardens were created on the site of the church and churchyard, although the removal of human remains did not take place until the new Peace Gardens were laid out in 1998. (*Author's Collection*)

Opposite, above: Barker's Pool viewed from Town Hall Square at the junction of Fargate and Leopold Street. With the exception of the building in the right foreground, immediately behind the statue, the remaining buildings were cleared to accommodate the Cinema House (opened 6 May 1913) and the City Hall (opened 22 September 1932). On one side of the stone plinth on which stands the statue of Queen Victoria are bronze figures representing 'Maternity'. A young woman holds a baby and her left arm is draped around the shoulders of a little girl. On the other side, clearly visible in this 1907 photograph, is the bronze figure representing 'Labour'. A young man, with shirt sleeves rolled up, sits on an anvil with a sledgehammer resting against his left inner leg. (*David J. Richardson Collection*)

Opposite, below: An Edwardian view of a bustling Pinstone Street and Town Hall Square. This postcard scene is franked 29 May 1905. (*Author's Collection*)

A *c.* 1910 postcard of Moorhead and Pinstone Street. The tower of St Paul's Church can be seen in the centre of the image. The monument, surrounded by iron railings, was erected on this site in 1863 to the designs of George Goldie, and commemorated servicemen who had died in the Crimean War. Its foundation stone had been laid in 1857 by His Royal Highness the Duke of Cambridge. The column was made of Aberdeen granite, with a stone base and capital. The seated figure which tops the monument represents 'Honour'. The Crimean War Memorial was removed in 1957 from Moorhead and placed, minus its column, in the Botanical Gardens. (*Author's Collection*)

Moorhead, 1970s. The Grosvenor House Hotel, in Charter Square, dominates the left skyline. This hotel was constructed during the 1960s, and part of the complex that surrounds its tower occupies the site of the Hippodrome (demolished 1963), whose entrance was in Cambridge Street, which runs off The Moor, second left. (*Author's Collection*)

Looking down The Moor from Moorhead. This postcard is franked 8 July 1968. Furnival Gate goes off to the left. (*Author's Collection*)

5

Around the City

Castle Market, on a card franked 22 June 1966.
This market, which opened in 1959, replaced the Norfolk Market Hall.
(Author's Collection)

An early 1960s postcard of the recently built Castle Market, seen from Waingate. Castle Market stands on the site of Sheffield Castle. The castle was demolished in 1648–9, leaving hardly a trace, when Parliament ordered that all castles which had been fortified by Royalists during the Civil War should be demolished. Part of what little remains of the castle can still be seen beneath the market complex. (*Author's Collection*)

Castle Market, Waingate, seen here in July 2000. (*Paul T. Langley Welch*)

Waingate, 1 June 2003. The Tap & Barrel pub, seen in the left foreground, stands at the corner of Castlegate. Sheffield's first town hall stood by the church gates in High Street. It was replaced in 1808 by the building seen here on the right side of Waingate, with its tower and clock. When the present town hall was completed it became the Court House. *(Keith Atack)*

Haymarket and beyond it, where the road bends, Waingate, 1979. A 'bendy bus', one of Sheffield's popular sights for over two decades, can be seen on the left. *(David J. Richardson Collection)*

The Pheasant Inn and Broad Street, *c.* 1890. The entire site became engulfed by the Sheaf Market shortly after this photograph was taken. A wholesale fish market opened on Shude Hill in 1879. By the middle of the decade that followed, the area adjacent to it was being used as an open air market selling such a wide range of goods that, although officially called the Sheaf Market, generations of Sheffielders referred to it as the 'Rag & Tag'. This market closed in 1973 and its trade transferred to the New Sheaf Market, built on the site of the old Castlefolds Market. That site has since been redeveloped. *(David J. Richardson Collection)*

An 1890s photo- graph taken from the roof of the Pheasant Inn, Broad Street. The Corn Exchange dominates the background. *(David J. Richardson Collection)*

This drawing of Old Pinfold Street is reproduced on a late Victorian postcard. The tower and dome of St Paul's Church can be seen in the right background. *(Author's Collection)*

Norfolk Street, 1933. The buildings seen here have long since gone. The Crucible Theatre, which opened in 1971, occupies the site today. *(David J. Richardson Collection)*

Commercial Street, 1902. The District Bank (later to become Barclays) building stands at the corner of Fitzalan Square. *(David J. Richardson Collection)*

Wicker Arches, July 1905. The Wicker and Wicker Arches have been decorated for the royal visit. The Lord Mayor of Sheffield, Herbert Hughes, can be seen wearing his mayoral robes in the left foreground. The origins of the name Wicker could lie in the old Norse word 'vikir', which means willow and 'carr' or 'kerr', a broad flat meadow. The Wicker was once meadowland and lies close to the River Don which, until its banks were crowded by breweries and steelworks, may well have been fringed with willow trees. *(David J. Richardson Collection)*

A postcard of the Wicker and Wicker Arches, *c.* 1907. *(Doreen Howse Collection)*

The Wicker and Wicker Arches, July 2000. *(Paul T. Langley Welch)*

A much less busy Wicker and Wicker Arches on the morning of 1 June 2003. *(Keith Atack)*

Pavement artists outside the Fitzalan Market, 1903. *(David J. Richardson Collection)*

6

Sheffield's
Brewing Industry

The names Sheaf Brewery and Ward's Brewery are proudly displayed above the
entrance portal in Eccleshall Road, May 1999. *(Keith Atack)*

Industrial expansion during the early part of the nineteenth century, ever on the increase in Sheffield, along with a rapidly growing population, resulted in an enormous number of pubs: around 1,500 licensed premises, according to the 1831 census. Sheffield's oldest brewery, founded in 1758, was Thos Rawson & Co. of Pond Street. To many steelworkers, the nature of their working environment meant that they were more than ready to slake their thirst with a pint or two of beer, once they had finished their shift. David Hey, in his book *A History of Sheffield* (1998), states, 'The heavy, hot nature of steelmaking made the workers in the east end legendary beer drinkers.' There was a fortune to be made in the brewing industry and several large breweries were built. In 1820, Proctor & Co. established their Exchange Brewery in the Market Place. This was taken over twenty years later by Edward and Robert Tennant, who moved the brewery to a site adjacent to Lady's Bridge, after they had sold their original premises to the Duke of Norfolk in order to build his market hall. This 1898 photograph taken from the bed of the River Don, shows Lady's Bridge and beyond it Tennants Exchange Brewery, with the attached Lady's Bridge Hotel. *(David J. Richardson Collection)*

A view of Lady's Bridge and the old Exchange Brewery from Blonk Street, July 2000. The Exchange Brewery closed in 1993. *(Paul T. Langley Welch)*

From modest beginnings in the 1840s, William Stones expanded his enterprises and in 1865 opened his Cannon Brewery in Rutland Road. Stones grew from strength to strength and their beers were very popular. The brewery was taken over by Bass in 1968. In November 1997 Bass announced that they were planning to buy Carlsberg-Tetley's brewery at Burton-on-Trent and close breweries in Cardiff and Sheffield, unless it could find buyers. Brewing of the Stones brand finally ceased at the Cannon Brewery in January 1999, when the brewery closed. The brand continues to be brewed by Coors Brewers Ltd at Burton-on-Trent, under licence from Interbrew UK. Seen here is the annual Horse Parade of William Stones Ltd, assembling outside the Cannon Brewery on 9 June 1902. *(Sheffield Central Library)*

By the 1880s there were thirty breweries of some size in Sheffield and numerous others operating on a smaller scale, often attached to public houses and brewing their beer largely, and in some instances exclusively, for in-house consumption. Of all the breweries that once proliferated, Ward's was probably one of the best known. In 1890 Septimus Henry Ward took over what had once been two breweries that had been brewing since the 1840s and merged by George Wright in the preceding decade (the Soho Brewery and the nearby Albion Brewery). The Sheaf Brewery, situated in the Eccleshall Road, continued to be run by Ward's until the brewery was taken over by Vaux in 1972. This famous Sunderland brewers kept Ward's Brewery as a subsidiary and traded under the same name. When Vaux itself was taken over by the Swallow Group, it was decided that both breweries and their associated pubs should be sold. An attempted management buyout failed and the pubs were sold off to Pubmaster Limited. Both the Vaux and Ward's breweries closed. Brewing of Ward's beers ceased on 2 June 1999. The entrance to Ward's Brewery is seen here shortly before its closure. *(Keith Atack)*

Ward's Brewery, seen here in May 1999. *(Keith Atack)*

Another view of the now demolished Ward's Brewery, also May 1999. *(Keith Atack)*

The Devonshire Arms, one of Ward's pubs, situated across from the brewery gates in Eccleshall Road, May 1999. *(Keith Atack)*

7

Industrial Sheffield

This postcard, captioned 'The Knife Grinders, Sheffield',
was posted in Hillsborough on 20 December 1909.
The message sent Christmas and New Year greetings from Mrs Hallam
to Mrs Barrowclough of Eversleigh Terrace, Herne Bay, Kent.
(Author's Collection)

The Clyde Steelworks of Samuel Osborn and Co. Ltd, a major employer of the time, on the banks of the River Don, *c.* 1900. The steelworks were situated between the Wicker and the River Don. The Royal Victoria Hotel can be seen on the right. *(David J. Richardson Collection)*

The Dannemora Steel Works, one of the many steelworks which were built right up to the banks of the River Don. *c.* 1900. *(David J. Richardson Collection)*

SHEFFIELD is the place to "SOOT" you.

This amusing postcard was sent during the First World War, in 1915. *(Author's Collection)*

An early postcard showing a typical Sheffield industrial scene. *(Author's Collection)*

White Rails on the banks of the River Don. Another early postcard view which only served to highlight the smoke-congested atmosphere of late nineteenth- and early twentieth-century Sheffield. *(Author's Collection)*

Making crucible steel at William Jessop & Sons Ltd, Brightside Works, *c.* 1904. *(Cyril Slinn Collection)*

Casting a large crucible steel ingot at William Jessop & Sons works. *(Cyril Slinn Collection)*

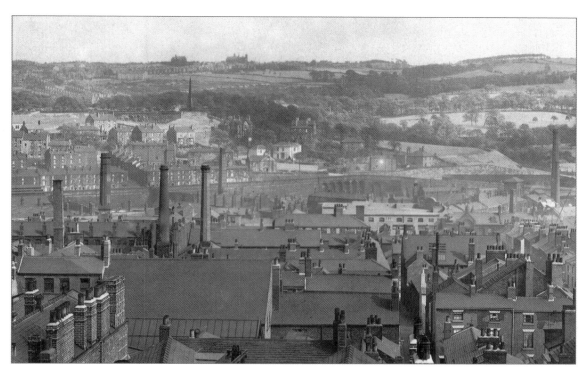

Sheffield roofscape, 1928. The Midland railway station can be seen centre right and beyond it Park Hill. *(David J. Richardson Collection)*

An aerial view of Sheffield, showing the beautiful countryside that surrounds what was at that time a heavily industrialised city, 1928. *(David J. Richardson Collection)*

A royal visit to Sheffield's steelworks, 1970s. HRH Prince Philip, Duke of Edinburgh, is seen here at Dunford Hadfields. On the left, wearing a safety helmet, is Mr Harold Short, safety and security manager. *(Courtesy of Harold Short)*

Joseph Elliot & Sons, cutlers, 1981. Mrs Gill is operating a pulling-on machine. *(Sheffield Central Library)*

Sheffield city centre, 1938. Frank Matcham's magnificent Empire Theatre can be seen in the bottom left-hand corner. Barker's Pool and the City Hall can be seen centre left and beyond it in the valley below can be seen some of the many industrial buildings that were scattered around the surrounding districts. *(David J. Richardson Collection)*

8

Composite Postcard Views

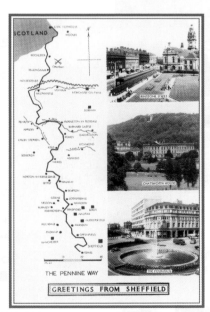

A composite card showing Sheffield's proximity
to the Pennine Way, 1965. *(Author's Collection)*

The Sheffield Telegraph building dominates the centre of these 1930s images of Sheffield. (*Author's Collection*)

An unusual 1930s good luck card, which features the recently opened City Hall and the extension to the Mappin Gallery. (*Author's Collection*)

This composite postcard, franked 19 May 1932, uses images taken early in the century, in the case of Sheffield Cathedral, and after 1913, in the case of Fargate. *(Author's Collection)*

A late 1930s composite featuring Barker's Pool Garden and St Paul's Gardens, formerly St Paul's churchyard, and shortly to become the Peace Gardens. *(Author's Collection)*

A 1940s Valentine's composite. *(Author's Collection)*

This composite was posted from Germany and sent to Sweden on 9 February 1961. *(Author's Collection)*

9

The Botanical Gardens

An early view of the Botanical Gardens, Broomhall.
(Author's Collection)

An early postcard featuring Sheffield's famous Botanical Gardens. The gardens, situated to the west of the city centre, cover a site of approximately 19 acres. They were laid out to the designs of Robert Marnock and opened in 1836. The Botanical Gardens were originally restricted to shareholders and subscribers, except on four gala days when the general public was admitted. *(Author's Collection)*

A lovely view of Sheffield Botanical Gardens, showing four little boys, all wearing hats. Three of them are dressed in sailor suits. *(Author's Collection)*

Sheffield Botanical Gardens, featuring the three pavilions designed by Sir Joseph Paxton (1801–65) in 1837. (*Author's Collection*)

A similar viewpoint to the one above. Among the attractions on offer in the gardens was the bear pit, which until the late nineteenth century was home to two brown bears. (*Author's Collection*)

An early view of Sheffield Botanical Gardens. Among the delights to be seen there were seasonally planted flower borders and beds, flowering shrubs, heath gardens and woodland areas. (*Author's Collection*)

10

Parks, Woods
& Gardens

This postcard showing the boating lake, Millhouses Park, is franked 25 August 1959. The 1860 Public Improvement Acts gave local authorities the power to acquire, create and manage parks out of the rates. Many such parks were opened throughout the country, some of them, such as Firth Park (see p. 86), donated by philanthropic individuals. *(Author's Collection)*

The boating lake at Forge Dam, Fulwood. The boathouse can be seen on the right. *(Author's Collection)*

An early panoramic postcard showing Forge Dam and Lake, Fulwood, and the surrounding area. *(Author's Collection)*

Crookes Valley Park and Dam, Crookesmoor. This postcard is franked 9 June 1909. *(Author's Collection)*

A pre-First World War postcard of Crookes Valley Recreation Ground, Crookesmoor. The recreation ground is situated on a site adjacent to Crookes Valley Park. This card is inscribed Private Walter Jenkins 12/15 Royal, and was presumably kept as a reminder of life back home. *(Author's Collection)*

The entrance gates of Norfolk Park. This postcard is franked 19 September 1906. Norfolk Park was one of the first public parks in the country, opened to the public in 1848 on land belonging to the Duke of Norfolk. It incorporates a main circular carriageway with two avenues, planted with lime trees and turkey oaks. *(Author's Collection)*

Another Edwardian postcard of the lodge and entrance gates at Norfolk Park. In 1897, when the Duke of Norfolk was Lord Mayor of Sheffield, Her Majesty Queen Victoria visited the city. She went to Norfolk Park, where schoolchildren sang to her. In 1910, the Duke of Norfolk gave the park to the City of Sheffield and a refreshment room was built to commemorate the event. *(Author's Collection)*

This postcard, franked 2 June 1935, shows the Pavilion, Graves Park. Graves Park, situated on the southern outskirts of the city, at a little over 200 acres, is Sheffield's largest park. The historic parkland had existed for centuries and was saved from development by Alderman J.G. Graves, a principal benefactor in Sheffield. He purchased the land in stages between 1926 and 1936, and Graves Park was created. He donated the park to the people of Sheffield to be kept as parkland in perpetuity. *(Author's Collection)*

This postcard, franked 10 July 1962, shows the beautifully stocked flower beds and manicured lawn in Graves Park. *(Author's Collection)*

An early twentieth-century view of the Lake, Hillsborough Park. (*Author's Collection*)

An early twentieth-century Valentine's postcard showing Beauchief Gardens. (*Author's Collection*)

This postcard, franked 24 August 1907, bears the inscription 'The Duck Pond, Firth Park'. This park, which covers 36 acres, was designed by Flockton and Abbott in 1874 and donated to the people of Sheffield by Mark Firth in 1875. The park was officially opened by His Royal Highness the Prince of Wales in that same year. What is described here as 'The Duck Pond' has also been used for sailing toy boats and as a paddling pool. The clocktower and refreshment rooms can be seen in the centre background. (*Author's Collection*)

A late Victorian postcard featuring the gates of Weston Park. *(Author's Collection)*

The gates of Weston Park about twenty years after the image above. Following the building of Sheffield University on the adjacent site, the height of the walls to the park has been increased, as can be seen by comparing the two pictures. *(Author's Collection)*

The Mappin Art Gallery, Weston Park, in a Valentine's postcard view of *c.* 1900. The gallery was built at a cost of £15,000 between 1886 and 1888, to the designs of architects Flockton & Gibbs. It has a long colonnaded front in the Ionic order and was founded under the terms of the will of John Newton Mappin, a wealthy cutlery manufacturer, who bequeathed 153 paintings. His nephew, Sir Frederick Mappin, presented a further 48, and other bequests followed. *(Author's Collection)*

A 1970s postcard view of the Mappin Art Gallery, Weston Park. *(Author's Collection)*

This view of the interior of the Mappin Art Gallery was produced by John Walsh Ltd, the famous Sheffield department store. It was posted to Canada on 13 September 1909. *(Author's Collection)*

An early twentieth-century postcard entitled 'In Weston Park, Sheffield'. *(Author's Collection)*

The War Memorial, Weston Park, is dedicated to the officers, NCOs and men of the York and Lancaster Regiment. An inscription shows that 8,814 men lost their lives (1914–19), as did 1,222 men from the regiment who fell (1939–45). Those additional figures were added to the memorial more than two decades after this postcard was produced. *(Author's Collection)*

The River Porter has its source in the moors above Sheffield and flows eastwards about 14 miles into the heart of the city. Its valley is a green corridor in which was created Bingham Park and on a site adjacent to Endcliffe Woods and on the opposite side of Rustlings Road to Bingham Park, Endcliffe Park, during the latter half of the nineteenth century. This late nineteenth-century postcard shows Endcliffe Park and the entrance to Endcliffe Woods. *(Author's Collection)*

The bridge across the River Porter and the drinking fountain by the entrance to Endcliffe Woods. *(Author's Collection)*

In the heart of Endcliffe Park, with the woods seen beyond. This postcard was sent in 1904. *(Author's Collection)*

This postcard, mailed on 4 March 1907, shows St Augustine's Church, from the viewpoint of Endcliffe Woods. *(Author's Collection)*

This card of Endcliffe Park and Woods is franked 15 January 1913. *(Author's Collection)*

This 1906 postcard is entitled 'Lake in Endcliffe Woods'. *(Author's Collection)*

This view, franked February 1911, is simply entitled 'Endcliffe, Sheffield'. *(Author's Collection)*

Another postcard franked 29 June 1904. This one bears the caption, 'The Dam, Endcliffe Woods, Sheffield'. *(Author's Collection)*

An early Valentine's series postcard entitled 'Stepping Stones, Endcliffe Woods'. (*Author's Collection*)

This postcard of the stepping stones at Endcliffe was published by the Loca-Vu Photo Co., Sheffield, and posted on 3 October 1913. (*Author's Collection*)

Yet another early postcard, photographed from an entirely different spot to the two images above, of the stepping stones in Endcliffe Woods. (*Author's Collection*)

An early postcard
showing the River Porter
and one of the weirs in
Endcliffe Woods.
(Author's Collection)

This early Valentine's
postcard gives a slightly
later view of the same
spot as the image above.
Their card is entitled
'Waterfall, Endcliffe
Woods, Sheffield'.
(Author's Collection)

Another early postcard of
Endcliffe Woods and the
River Porter. *(Author's
Collection)*

One of the crossing points of the River Porter, in the heart of Endcliffe Woods. *(Author's Collection)*

The Park House, Tea Room and shop, Endcliffe Park, 22 April 2003. The statue of Queen Victoria can be seen to the right. *(Keith Atack)*

Queen Victoria's statue by Alfred Turner (1904) was moved to Endcliffe Park in 1930 (for a full description see pp. 46 and 48). *(Keith Atack)*

This early postcard of the Ruskin Museum, Meersbrook Park, is franked 22 August 1905. John Ruskin (1821–1900), poet, writer and art critic, was the son of a prosperous London wine merchant. He attended Christ Church, Oxford, graduating with an MA in 1843. He soon gained a reputation as a brilliant art critic. After meeting the painter J.M.W. Turner (1775–1851), he championed that artist's works in his first critical work, *Modern Painters* (1843–60). This book, along with *The Seven Lamps of Architecture* (1848) and *The Stones of Venice* (1851–3), raised him to the status of the most celebrated critic of his day. Ruskin also championed the young Pre-Raphaelites. He became Professor of Fine Arts at Oxford in 1870. Ruskin is considered to have been one of that group of Englishmen who began the Arts and Crafts movement. He held radical views and nurtured a particular dislike for classical works in buildings and in art. Ruskin founded the Guild of St George in 1871, a body which existed to further these beliefs. He first visited Sheffield in 1875, when the Guild founded the St George's Museum, at Walkley. It was one of four such sites founded by Ruskin through the Guild of St George. The museum in Sheffield housed a collection arranged by Ruskin. Originally contained in one room, the collection included books, prints, illuminated manuscripts, drawings, plaster casts, mineral and geological specimens and coins. As the collection grew the site at the cottage in Walkley became too small and the collection was moved in 1890 to the building in Meersbrook Park, seen here. Ruskin wrote, 'In all museums intended for popular teaching, there are two great evils to be avoided. The first is superabundance; the second, disorder. The first is having too much of everything. You will find in your own work that the less you have to look at, the better you attend. You can no more see twenty things worth seeing in an hour, than you can read twenty books worth reading in a day. Give little, but that little good and beautiful, and explain it thoroughly.' In 1963 the collection was moved to the University of Reading but was returned to Sheffield when the renamed Ruskin Gallery opened in Norfolk Street in 1985. The Ruskin Gallery closed in December 2000 in preparation for yet another move and a spring 2001 opening in the Millennium Galleries. The building seen in this image is now offices for the Parks Department of Sheffield City Council. (*Author's Collection*)

11

Celebrated Beauty Spots

A post-Second World War composite postcard
of some of Sheffield's beauty spots. (*Author's Collection*)

This Bamforth composite postcard is franked 25 April 1957. *(Author's Collection)*

One of the Bamforth views featured in the previous composite, entitled 'View from the Surprise, Sheffield'. *(Author's Collection)*

An early postcard scene featuring Whiteley Wood and the River Porter, franked 8 October 1910. *(Author's Collection)*

This early postcard, sent to New Zealand on 18 April 1907, bears the inscription 'Waterfall, Whiteley Woods, Sheffield'. *(Author's Collection)*

A view from the Reliable series of postcards of Whiteley Woods, sent to Miss G. Mumford, c/o Mr Woodhouse, Manor House, Hexthorpe, Doncaster, and franked 3 January 1906. *(Author's Collection)*

This Kromo series postcard view of Whiteley Woods was posted on 15 August 1918 in Heeley and sent to Bournemouth. *(Author's Collection)*

An early postcard entitled 'The Waterfall, Whiteley Woods, Sheffield', and posted in 1905. Those were more innocent times when local post offices knew their residents. The card is simply addressed to Miss Maddy c/o Mrs Marling, Clanna, Lydney, Gloucestershire. *(Author's Collection)*

A lovely early view of a horse and trap crossing the River Porter, in Whiteley Woods. This postcard is franked 30 July 1905. *(Author's Collection)*

An early postcard produced by G. Bagshaw & Son of 549 Eccleshall Road. It shows the Old Forge House in Whiteley Woods, which was used as refreshment rooms (as shown in the composite on p. 100). *(Author's Collection)*

Bolsover Dam, Whiteley Woods. This postcard is franked 12 August 1948. *(Author's Collection)*

This postcard, one of the Royal York series, published by W.H.S. & S. Sheffield, was sent as a Christmas greeting with the message 'With best wishes for a merry Christmas and a Happy New Year, from us all', without any clue to who was sending it, to Mr and Mrs E.C. Barker, Mount Pleasant, Newcastle-under-Lyne, Staffs, and posted on 24 December 1904. It is captioned 'Convalescent Hospital, Whiteley Woods, Sheffield'. The building is in fact the George Woofindin Convalescent Home, which opened in Whiteley Woods in 1901. *(Author's Collection)*

An early twentieth-century composite postcard showing the various delights to be seen at Wyming Brook, situated to the east of the city. *(Author's Collection)*

An Edwardian postcard view entitled 'New Drive through Wyming Brook, Sheffield'. *(Author's Collection)*

A post-First World War postcard published by R. Sneath of Paradise Street, entitled 'Wyming Brook, Sheffield'. It is franked 5 September 1927. (*Author's Collection*)

'In Wyming Brook'. Another Sneath postcard view. (*Author's Collection*)

Another from the Sneath stable of cards of Wyming Brook. (*Author's Collection*)

This postcard of Wyming Brook is franked 17 January 1927. (*Author's Collection*)

An unusually uninspiring Sneath postcard featuring Wyming Brook once more. It is not really much of a view but an interesting composition of water, rocks, grass and bracken. (*Author's Collection*)

Deep in the woods in Wyming Brook. A Sneath postcard of what was, during the first quarter of the twentieth century, rapidly becoming one of Sheffield's most popular beauty spots. (*Author's Collection*)

The wooded slopes at the eastern edge of Wyming Brook. Sneath postcards were very popular in the early twentieth century. (*Author's Collection*)

An Edwardian postcard of Wyming Ravine. *(Author's Collection)*

This postcard, franked 11 June 1934, is entitled, 'Hollow Meadows, Wyming Brook, Sheffield'. The wooded slopes of Wyming Brook open out to magnificent views of the Hollow Meadow Dams in the Rivelin Valley. *(Author's Collection)*

This card, 'Among the Pines, Wyming Brook, Sheffield', was posted to the Isle of Wight in March 1915. *(Author's Collection)*

This card of 'New Road, Wyming Brook, Sheffield' was published by the Loca-Vu Photo Co. and was posted to Bury St Edmunds on 23 February 1916. *(Author's Collection)*

Posted on 26 July 1920, this postcard is entitled 'Wyming Brook, New Road'. *(Author's Collection)*

An early twentieth-century postcard photographed from the wooded slopes of Wyming Brook, across Wyming New Road to the Hollow Meadow Dams. *(Author's Collection)*

This Valentine's series postcard, franked 10 September 1923, and entitled 'Wyming Brook Valley, Sheffield', shows the magnificent view to be afforded. *(Author's Collection)*

Wharncliffe Crags, situated north-west of Sheffield. Before road and rail transport made travelling to more distant attractions easier to reach, Wharncliffe Crags was a popular place to visit for the people of Sheffield and the surrounding areas, particularly at Easter and Whitsuntide, when it was not unusual for there to be hundreds of visitors. Today the crags are mostly visited by hikers and climbers. *(Author's Collection)*

An early twentieth-century view of Wharncliffe Crags, which helps to illustrate just how popular an attraction they were. *(Chris Sharp of Old Barnsley)*

This early twentieth-century Scott postcard shows 'The Lodge, Wharncliffe Crags'. Wharncliffe Lodge was built in the early sixteenth century on top of a crag in the savage wilderness of Wharncliffe Chase. An inscription carved on a nearby rock and recorded in *Some Account of English Deer* by E.P. Shirley, published in 1807, asks the reader to pray for the soul of Sir Thomas Wortley, 'which caused a lodge to be made on this crag in the midst of Wharncliffe for his pleasure to hear the hart's bell [the stag's rutting cry], in the year of our Lord 1510.' *(Author's Collection)*

This Scott Russell & Co. postcard showing the beautiful 'Cordwell Valley, near Sheffield', is franked 28 September 1907. *(Author's Collection)*

An early Kromo series postcard of the Loxley Valley. *(Author's Collection)*

This postcard shows the tranquil Loxley Valley during the early twentieth century. *(Author's Collection)*

This early Valentine's postcard of 'Old Mill, Rivelin Valley, Sheffield', was sent to Sapper T.E. Williams, 304309, Royal Engineers, at Christchurch, Hants, on 11 September 1917. *(Author's Collection)*

This Valentine's series postcard, franked 6 August 1919, shows Upper Cut Mill, Rivelin Valley. The River Rivelin rises in the Hallam moors, north-west of Sheffield. The Rivelin is joined by the River Loxley at Malin Bridge before flowing into the River Don at Hillsborough. *(Author's Collection)*

A Sneath postcard entitled 'Rivelin Valley, Sheffield', postmarked 11 September 1911. *(Author's Collection)*

The Rivelin Valley, franked 10 September 1925. *(Author's Collection)*

This Kromo series postcard, entitled 'Rivelin Waterfall, Sheffield', is franked 16 January 1911. *(Author's Collection)*

This Peak series postcard, published by R. Sneath, Devonshire Street, Sheffield, of the New Road, Rivelin, Sheffield, is franked 21 January 1913. It was sent to Miss Brooke, Valley Farm, Ashton-under-Lyne, and informs 'My Dear Mary' that 'this is another part of the New Road'. *(Author's Collection)*

This early postcard, published in the J.W.M & R.P.S. series, Sheffield, is entitled, 'Old Machon on Bank, Sheffield'. *(Author's Collection)*

12

Images around Sheffield

The interior of St John the Evangelist Church, Ranmoor,
posted in January 1913. The church was constructed in the late
thirteenth-century style to the designs of Flockton & Gibbs, 1887–8.
(Author's Collection)

Sheffield University, c. 1914. Sir Marcus Samuel Bt (later Lord Bearsted), Lord Mayor of London, laid the foundation stone of the university buildings in 1903. Constructed to the designs of architect E. Michael Gibbs, Sheffield University was opened by Their Majesties King Edward VII and Queen Alexandra, on 12 July 1905. *(Author's Collection)*

An Edwardian postcard of Sheffield University, franked 21 August 1910, seen from Weston Park. *(Author's Collection)*

Sheffield University, 1970s. *(Author's Collection)*

The old Sheffield
Polytechnic building (now
Sheffield's second
university, Hallam) in Pond
Street, seen in July 2000.
(Paul T. Langley Welch)

This early postcard of Wesley College is franked 9 January 1905. The Revd Samuel Dousland Waddy (1804–76), a Wesleyan minister, decided that Sheffield needed a superior school to give boys a classical education and teach them the principles of Methodism. He was supported by members of Sheffield's Wesleyan community and a building committee was formed. Land was purchased from William Newbould in 1836, which comprised 5 acres, 2 roods and 20 perches, for £4,218 18s. Sheffield architect William Flockton designed the building, which has the appearance of a large country house. Construction took over a year and a half and the total cost of buying the land, putting up the buildings and surrounding walls, and buying furnishings, amounted to £27,696 11s 9½d. The school accepted its first intake of 90 boarders on 8 August 1838. By 1841 there were 172 pupils. In 1905 Wesley College and Sheffield Royal Grammar School merged, and the name was changed to King Edward VII School. Fees were abolished in 1945 and the school continued to operate as a boys' grammar school until in 1969 Crosspool Secondary School amalgamated with it. The school is now a mixed comprehensive, taking pupils from the age of eleven to eighteen. *(Author's Collection)*

An Edwardian view of Fulwood Road. Ranmoor. The spire of St John the Evangelist (see p. 119) can be seen in the distance on the right-hand side of the road. *(Author's Collection)*

A cold day in Crookes, 1906. *(Doreen Howse Collection)*

The Market Cross, Woodhouse, *c.* 1900. *(Chris Sharp of Old Barnsley)*

An early twentieth-century view of bank corner (named after the Yorkshire Bank) at the junction of Burncross Road with Station Road, Chapeltown. *(Author's Collection)*

The junction of Burncross Road and Station Road, Chapeltown, 22 June 2003. *(Keith Atack)*

St Thomas Becket's Church, Beauchief. This image shows part of the west end of Beauchief Abbey, founded in about 1175, and incorporated into the church seen here. Once situated in splendid isolation, Beauchief Abbey has been hemmed in by the sprawl of Sheffield's suburbs. Fortunately a golf course preserves some of the open landscape that still surrounds this semi-ruin. *(Author's Collection)*

Ye Old Cross Scythes Hotel, Totley, *c.* 1900. *(Chris Sharp of Old Barnsley)*

Dore, one of Sheffield's loveliest villages, seen here during the early twentieth century. *(Chris Sharp of Old Barnsley)*

St Thomas's Church, Wincobank, *c.* 1910. The church was built in Newman Road in 1875. Its appearance belies its age, possibly because of the clever use of materials and the industrial grime that has hastened the mellowing of the stonework. Unlike many churches erected throughout England during that period, St Thomas's gives the impression that it has been standing for centuries. *(Chris Sharp of Old Barnsley)*

The Norfolk Arms, Penistone Road, Grenoside, situated at the edge of the village close to Greno Wood. In this late Victorian scene two ladies are setting out in their pony-trap. *(Chris Sharp of Old Barnsley)*

The small village of Wharncliffe Side, *c.* 1920. Wharncliffe Side, where file cutters once plied their trade, is situated 6 miles to the north-north-west of Sheffield, in the valley nestling beneath Wharncliffe Crags (see p. 112) and forming part of the Wharncliffe Estate. Wharncliffe Side is a community of just over 2,500 people. *(Chris Sharp of Old Barnsley)*

An Edwardian view of Oughtibridge. Taken from Station Lane, this image shows the magnificent countryside that completely surrounds the village. *(Chris Sharp of Old Barnsley)*

St Nicholas's Church, Bradfield, *c.* 1905. Situated in High Bradfield, this church was erected in 1109 by the Lovetot family, who had become lords of the manor during the reign of William the Conqueror. The Lovetots also built St Mary's Church, Ecclesfield (see p. 2), to whose enormous parish this church became a chapel-of-ease until 1868. A square belltower was added to the Norman structure in the fourteenth century before the church was enlarged and remodelled in the Gothic Perpendicular style in the fifteenth. On the right can be seen a charming watch-house, built in 1831 by concerned local citizens, to safeguard newly buried bodies from being stolen by resurrectionists, the unscrupulous body-snatchers, and taken to the medical schools in Sheffield to be dissected by tutor surgeons. The Anatomy Act of 1839 quickly brought an end to this practice. *(Chris Sharp of Old Barnsley)*

Situated above Stocksbridge, the village of Bolsterstone stands 984ft above sea level and is surrounded by spectacular scenery. A few fragments of the castle built by the Sheffield family in 1250 remain nearby. The Castle Inn, which stands next to the church, was once owned by the celebrated performer Sam Costa, well known for his radio broadcasts, including ITMA. Bolsterstone has had a succession of churches since the twelfth century. The present St Mary's was built in 1879. A list of incumbents is displayed in the church dating from 1412 to the present day. *(Chris Sharp of Old Barnsley)*

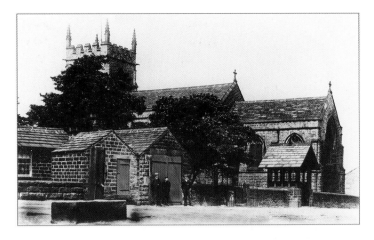

The LMS (London, Midland & Scottish), *Princess Elizabeth* (no. 42601, William Stanier locomotive), steaming through Millhouses on 2 June 1990. *(Keith Atack)*

Wadsley parish church. Built in 1834 through the generosity of the Misses Harrison, it was partly destroyed by fire in 1884 and reopened the following year. *(Chris Sharp of Old Barnsley)*

ACKNOWLEDGEMENTS

Mrs Iris Ackroyd, Vera Atack, Anne Bennett, Mrs Joan Bostwick, Tony Briggs, Tracy P. Deller, Ricky S. Deller, Miss Joanna C. Murray Deller, the Director of Legal and Administrative Services (Sheffield City Council), Annabel Fearnley, Simon Fletcher, Andy Gaffey, Doug Hindmarch, Senior Local Studies Librarian at Sheffield Central Library, Mrs Ann Howse, Mrs Doreen Howse, Mrs Kathleen Howse, Chris Sharp of Old Barnsley, Harold Short, Cyril Slinn, Mr David Walker and Mrs Christine Walker of Walkers Newsagents, Hoyland, Mr Ivan P. Walker, Miss Suki B. Walker, Stuart Webb (Sheffield City Council), Mr Clifford Willoughby, Mrs Margaret Willoughby.

I would like to thank John D. Murray, who has assisted me over many years.

I am particularly grateful to David J. Richardson for use of images from his extensive photographic collection and to Paul T. Langley Welch and Keith Atack, who have photographed some of the more recent images of Sheffield.

The Coat of Arms of Sheffield is reproduced by kind permission of the City Council but does not represent an endorsement of this book by the Council. The Coat of Arms of Sheffield should NOT be used without the Council's permission.

Tinsley Viaduct and the Ml motorway, seen here from above Meadowhall in the 1970s. *(Keith Atack)*